I Love You No Matter What

by Patti Rey

Illustrated by Dany Gutierrez

Jesus came down from Heaven and lived on Earth.
He is called Immanuel which means God with us.
He taught many things including love, kindness,
and forgiveness.

He knows we are not perfect and that we will make
mistakes. "But God demonstrates his own love for us
in this: While we were still sinners, Christ died for us."
Romans 5:8 NIV

Through believing in Jesus and telling Him you are
sorry, you are forgiven when you hurt another or
do something wrong.

Always try to do good, but know in your heart
you are <u>always</u> loved by God!

He loves you... no matter what!

Through your good days
Hasta en tus días buenos

and bad days,
y tus días malos,

your happy
en tus felices

and sad days,
y días tristes,

I love you
¡Te amo

no matter what!
no importa que!

Always know
Sabes que siempre

no matter how your day goes,
no importando como vaya tu día,

I love you
no matter what!

¡Te amo
no importa que!

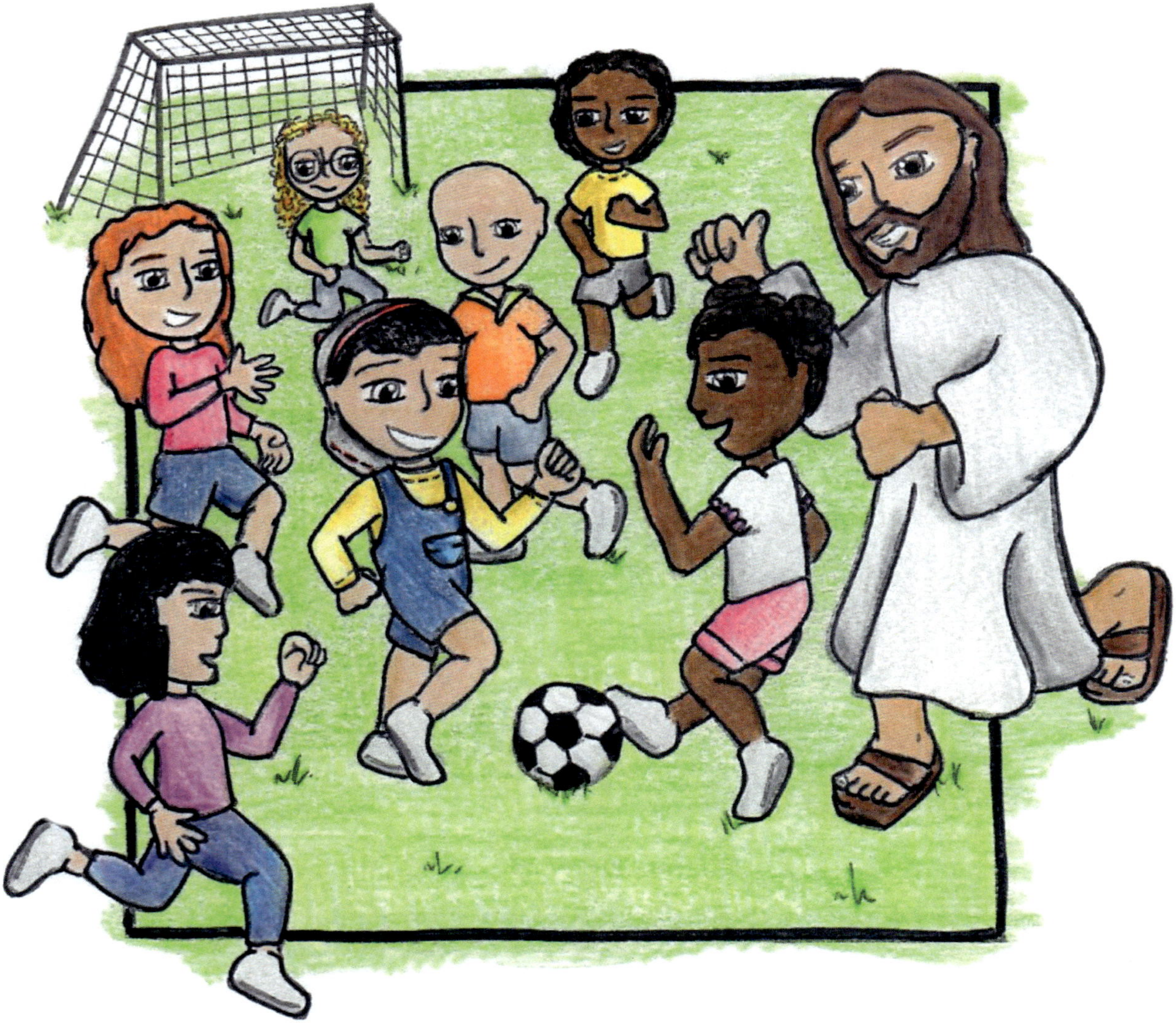

Whatever comes your way
Lo que sea que se te presente

know I'll always stay
sabes que siempre estaré

right here beside you,
justo aquí a tu lado

always willing to guide you.
siempre dispuesto a guiarte.

I love you
no matter what!

¡Te amo
no importa que!

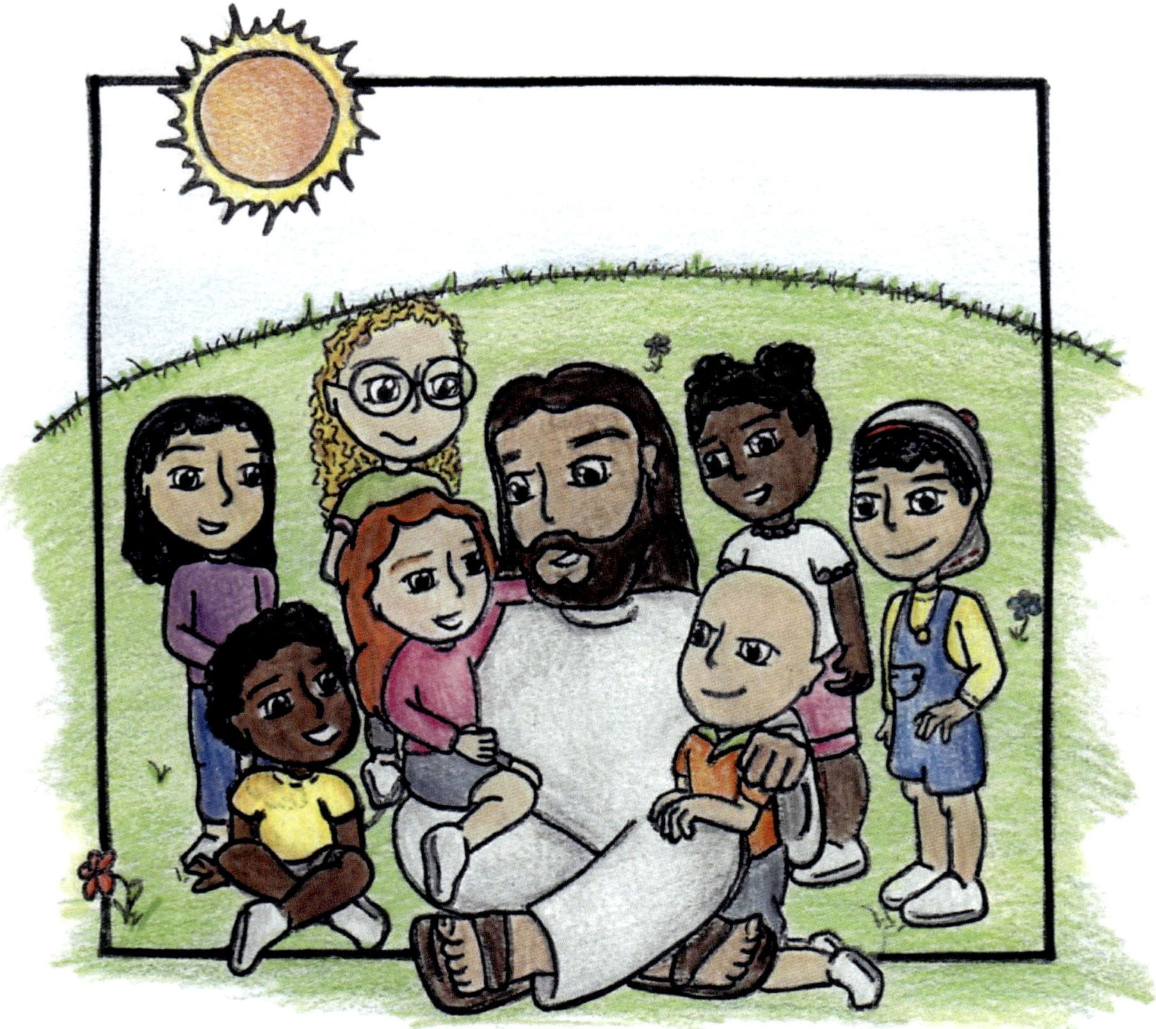

No Matter What
Julie Burgart

No mat-ter what,___ (Clap! Clap!) I love you no mat-ter what.___ (Clap! Clap!)
No im-por-ta que (¡Aplauso! ¡Aplauso!) te a-mo no im-por-ta que (¡Aplauso! ¡Aplauso!)

Al - ways know no mat-ter how your day goes, I love you no mat-ter what.___
No importan - do co-mo va - ya tu día te a-mo no im - por-ta que.

Through your good days___ and bad___ days, your hap - py and your sad, sad days,
En - tus dí - as buenos y días malos en - los fe - lices y dí - as tristes

Al - ways know no mat-ter how your day goes, I love you no mat-ter what. ___ No mat-ter what,
No importan - do co-mo va - ya tu día te amo no im-porta que No importa que

___ (Clap! Clap!) I love you no mat-ter what.___ (Clap! Clap!) Al - ways know no mat-ter
(¡Aplauso! ¡Aplauso!) te a-mo no im - por-ta que (¡Aplauso! ¡Aplauso!) No impor - tan - do co-mo

how your day goes, I love you no mat-ter what.___ Through what-ev - er___
va - ya tu día te a-mo no im-por-ta que.___ Lo que se-a que ven-ga

Thank you to the talented Dany Gutierrez for the beautiful illustrations, Maria Rosa Gutierrez for translating so we can spread this message far and wide, Julie Burgart for composing a lively little song to accompany the book, and Samantha Biersner for her many hours of graphic design and pre-press work at Strategic Imaging. Thank You, God, for letting me play a part in getting this message to Your children - what a joy!

Learn Spanish
What do the following words mean?
If you need help – look back through the book.

días buenos

felices

te amo

guiarte

no importa que

siempre

Practice the following English sight words.

I	you	good
what	and	to

What letter does the picture start with?
Trace with your finger to find the answer.

Find and Seek
Look through the book and find the following objects.

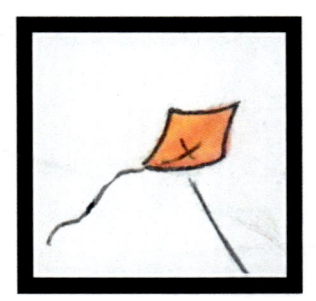

Pattern Game
Notice the pattern. What comes next?

Azariah, you are an incredible gift. God loves you so much and has big plans for you. :)

Meet the Illustrator

Dany Gutierrez

Dany Gutierrez

Dany was a Junior in High School when she illustrated this book. Having grown up surrounded by both artistic and religious parents she has created a passion for drawing and serving the Lord. Throughout her life, Dany has always been fascinated by Disney and the messages that can be created by animation, and hopes to one day be able to do the same.

Meet the Author

Patti Rey

Patti was "made new in Christ" in 2014. Since then, Spirit has been using her to share poems, prayers, and messages via social media. God gifted her with a #1 ranking on Amazon in August of 2018 with her first book *Inspirations and Praise*. Due to her passion to reach all ages, she began writing children's books in that same year. In addition to writing, Patti is also a motivational speaker, always eager to share what Spirit has placed on her heart. She resides in Iowa with her college sweetheart, Mike. God has blessed them with three wonderful sons, Tanner, Zach, and Austin.

Made in the USA
Columbia, SC
11 August 2019